Instant Brainshark

Convert your boring, outdated slideshows into engaging and powerful audio presentations using Brainshark

Daniel Li

PUBLISHING

BIRMINGHAM - MUMBAI

Instant Brainshark

First published: September 2013

Production Reference: 1230913

Published by Packt Publishing Ltd.
Livery Place
35 Livery Street
Birmingham B3 2PB, UK.

ISBN 978-1-78355-926-8

www.packtpub.com

Credits

Author
Daniel Li

Reviewer
Karen Bieger

Acquisition Editor
Saleem Ahmed

Mary Nadar

Commissioning Editor
Yogesh Dalvi

Technical Editor
Mrunmayee Patil

Project Coordinator
Romal Karani

Proofreader
Stephen Copestake

Graphics
Ronak Dhruv

Production Coordinator
Aparna Bhagat

Cover Work
Aparna Bhagat

Cover Image
Valentina Dsilva

About the Author

Daniel Li is an independent consultant for small and medium-sized businesses, currently residing in Waterloo, Ontario. Having paid experience at over a dozen institutions since 2009, he leverages his marketing and sales experience as a startup advisor in writing this book. Having placed first in the International NEO Coding Competition while spending three years contributing to the open-source community, he earned a placement as a "Canada's Top 20 Under 20 2013" finalist. He also occasionally answers questions on the collaborative Q&A website, Stackoverflow.com, as a top 4% user.

I would like to dedicate this book to all those who believed in me.

About the Reviewer

Karen Bieger is an educator with professional experience spanning 20 years in both corporate and academic environments. She earned her Bachelor's in Education at Thomas More College in Kentucky, and her Master's Degree in Administration and Supervision at Butler University, Indiana. She continued graduate work in Instructional Leadership at Xavier University in Cincinnati, OH. After working as a Teacher and Principal in elementary schools while living in the Midwest and southern United States, she now designs and delivers instruction as a Corporate Trainer and Instructional Designer. Professional environments have included A.C. Nielsen, Macy's, Pepsi-Cola and The Kroger Company. Her presentation style features participant interaction and practical examples that can be readily applied in the workplace. She facilitates training in person as well as through distance learning to international clients.

www.PacktPub.com

Support files, eBooks, discount offers, and more

You might want to visit www.PacktPub.com for support files and downloads related to your book.

Did you know that Packt offers eBook versions of every book published, with PDF and ePub files available? You can upgrade to the eBook version at www.PacktPub.com and as a print book customer, you are entitled to a discount on the eBook copy. Get in touch with us at service@packtpub.com for more details.

At www.PacktPub.com, you can also read a collection of free technical articles, sign up for a range of free newsletters and receive exclusive discounts and offers on Packt books and eBooks.

http://PacktLib.PacktPub.com

Do you need instant solutions to your IT questions? PacktLib is Packt's online digital book library. Here, you can access, read and search across Packt's entire library of books.

Why Subscribe?

- ▸ Fully searchable across every book published by Packt
- ▸ Copy and paste, print and bookmark content
- ▸ On demand and accessible via web browser

Free Access for Packt account holders

If you have an account with Packt at www.PacktPub.com, you can use this to access PacktLib today and view nine entirely free books. Simply use your login credentials for immediate access.

Table of Contents

Preface

Today's fast-paced business environment has led to the emergence of more efficient presentation platforms. Brainshark's cloud-based storage and audio capabilities allow the acceleration of your sales cycle like never before, integrating smoothly into your existing processes. In addition, its mobile app allows your staff, co-workers, or clients to view presentations on-the-go, a must-have feature to accommodate everyone's busy schedule. This book will cover the knowledge required to use Brainshark as a presentation platform as well as best practices to ensure an optimal amount of sales conversions.

What this book covers

Creating your first presentation (Must know), will show readers how to start their first presentation, with content design tips to enhance their sales cycle using Brainshark's audio annotation system. It will also show a step-by-step process on how to delete and print presentations after creation.

Increasing sales with Brainshark slideshows/documents (Become an expert), will show step-by-step recipes on how to ergonomically design presentations for sales conversions. It will also cover details regarding basic aesthetic appeal tips.

Increasing sales with Brainshark podcasts (Become an expert), will similarly illustrate the best practices involved in podcast presentations to increase conversion rates. It will go over the must-have components of any podcast announcer including transcripts and audio equipment.

Helping people find your presentation (Should know), will include a step-by-step explanation on how to properly tag presentations using Brainshark. It will also include details on how to properly assign a category for a presentation using Brainshark. It will also include a brief introduction to search engine optimization, assuming no knowledge, to help illustrate the importance of presentation tags and categories.

Designing mobile-friendly presentations (Become an expert), will show a step-by-step process to install the Brainshark mobile application in order to allow for self-testing. It will also demonstrate how to create mobile-friendly presentations alongside a step-by-step guide on how to test them using Brainshark's mobile applications. Lastly, it will show you how to disable mobile functionality if it is unnecessary for the presentation.

Synchronizing slide animations to audio (Should know), will show a step-by-step process on how to sync slide animations with Brainshark. It will follow this up with slide animations that fail to sync with audio and best practices to avoid this from occurring. Lastly, the chapter will delve into editing and deleting slide animations after the presentation has been published.

Adding PowerPoint slides (Must know), will show how to upload a PowerPoint slide for a given slide presentation. This section will demonstrate the best practices in adding slides for a given presentation and will also show how to remove slides that you have just added in.

Adding URL slides (Become an expert), will show how to fully utilize URL slide functionality. It will cover how to work with the web URL slides and edit the contents of your presentations on the fly by changing your website instead of all your presentations.

Adding question slides (Become an expert), will show a step-by-step process on how to add a question slide. The chapter will then demonstrate best practices in designing a question slide with carefully chosen responses. Lastly, it will go over the importance of customer feedback to further emphasize the use of question slides.

Adding attachments (Must know), will discuss valid file types for attachment. Then, it will show a step-by-step process on how to add valid attachments. Lastly, it will demonstrate how to remove an attachment once it has been uploaded.

Embedding your content (Should know), will show a step-by-step process on how to embed content on a website. The chapter will then demonstrate how to use QR codes to embed content for mobile devices.

E-mailing your content (Become an expert), will discuss the various ways to share a presentation over the web using e-mail. The chapter will talk briefly about Brainshark's e-mail spam policy and best practices in maintaining the shared content.

Sharing your content (Become an expert), will demonstrate how to share content via social media using Brainshark's sharing tools. It will then conclude by including some tips on how to properly harness the power of social media.

Publishing your content to YouTube (Become an expert), will show a step-by-step process on how to sync a presentation to your YouTube account through Brainshark. It will then proceed to explain how the conversion process works and how the ownership of the content transfers.

What you need for this book

You will need a MyBrainshark individual account in order to fully utilize the software involved. The *Creating your first presentation* recipe will cover the details of how to attain an account. You may also optionally wish to attain a smartphone to test your presentations using Brainshark's premier mobile app.

Who this book is for

This book is for those who actively create or showcase sales presentations for a particular product. This includes sales agents, account executives, entrepreneurs, and consultants. As this book covers internet marketing practices alongside tips for sales conversions, it can also be leveraged as a guide for online presentations in general.

Conventions

In this book, you will find a number of styles of text that distinguish between different kinds of information. Here are some examples of these styles, and an explanation of their meaning.

Code words in text are shown as follows: "We can include other contexts through the use of the include directive."

New terms and **important words** are shown in bold. Words that you see on the screen, in menus or dialog boxes for example, appear in the text like this: "Select the **Next** button and it will undergo the Brainshark conversion process".

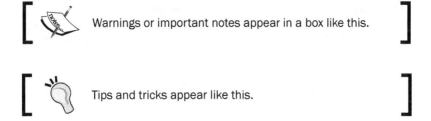

Warnings or important notes appear in a box like this.

Tips and tricks appear like this.

Reader feedback

Feedback from our readers is always welcome. Let us know what you think about this book—what you liked or may have disliked. Reader feedback is important for us to develop titles that you really get the most out of.

To send us general feedback, simply send an e-mail to feedback@packtpub.com, and mention the book title via the subject of your message.

If there is a book that you need and would like to see us publish, please send us a note in the **SUGGEST A TITLE** form on www.packtpub.com or e-mail suggest@packtpub.com.

If there is a topic that you have expertise in and you are interested in either writing or contributing to a book, see our author guide on www.packtpub.com/authors.

Customer support

Now that you are the proud owner of a Packt book, we have a number of things to help you to get the most from your purchase.

Errata

Although we have taken every care to ensure the accuracy of our content, mistakes do happen. If you find a mistake in one of our books—maybe a mistake in the text or the code—we would be grateful if you would report this to us. By doing so, you can save other readers from frustration and help us improve subsequent versions of this book. If you find any errata, please report them by visiting http://www.packtpub.com/support, selecting your book, clicking on the **errata submission form** link, and entering the details of your errata. Once your errata are verified, your submission will be accepted and the errata will be uploaded on our website, or added to any list of existing errata, under the Errata section of that title. Any existing errata can be viewed by selecting your title from http://www.packtpub.com/support.

Piracy

Piracy of copyright material on the Internet is an ongoing problem across all media. At Packt, we take the protection of our copyright and licenses very seriously. If you come across any illegal copies of our works, in any form, on the Internet, please provide us with the location address or website name immediately so that we can pursue a remedy.

Please contact us at copyright@packtpub.com with a link to the suspected pirated material.

We appreciate your help in protecting our authors, and our ability to bring you valuable content.

Questions

You can contact us at questions@packtpub.com if you are having a problem with any aspect of the book, and we will do our best to address it.

Instant Brainshark

Welcome to *Instant Brainshark*. Today's fast-paced business environment has led to the emergence of more efficient presentation platforms. Brainshark's cloud-based storage and audio capabilities allow the acceleration of your sales cycle as never before, integrating smoothly into your existing processes. The emergence of smartphones has led to an additional platform for viewing presentations online. Brainshark's mobile application allows your staff, co-workers, or clients to view presentations on-the-go, at their own convenience. This book will cover the knowledge required to use Brainshark as a presentation platform, as well as best practices to ensure an optimal amount of sales conversions.

The first part of the book will aid you in getting started with Brainshark. As you proceed further, the book will cover the details on how to get the most out of the presentation software in the various situations described.

Creating your first presentation (Must know)

We will first look into the basics of using Brainshark by exploring the fundamentals. By learning how to create your first presentation, you can easily move onto the more advanced sections, illustrating how to add, edit, and delete various types of content in your presentation.

An example of a Brainshark presentation

Getting ready

Through this recipe, we will be able to start our first presentation, with content design tips to enhance your sales cycle using Brainshark's audio annotation system. To start, you should ideally prepare some file(s) in one of the valid formats, depending on the type of presentation you're seeking to create:

Narrated slideshow presentations

Narrated slideshow presentations represent the core functionality of Brainshark. By importing your existing slideshows, you may add audio annotations, enhancing your audience's experience. We will cover more on these presentations in future recipes.

Valid formats include:

- ► `.ppt`/`.pptx`: Microsoft PowerPoint slideshows
- ► `.odp`: Open Office presentation format

Photo albums

Photo albums allow you to share image content in a presentable manner over the Internet. Whether you wish to showcase vacation photos to your friends or family, or even promote the sale of your product via images, photo albums are a great way to deliver your content.

Valid formats include:

- ► `.jpg`/`.jpeg`: JPEG image file
- ► `.gif`: GIF image file
- ► `.png`: PNG image file
- ► `.bmp`: Bitmap image file

Video presentations

You may also choose to upload existing video files to play on Brainshark. This may be ideal for when you wish to internally link a video from an existing Brainshark presentation or show off a product in real time.

Valid formats include:

- ► `.avi`: AVI video file
- ► `.flv`: Flash video file
- ► `.mov`: QuickTime movie file
- ► `.wmv`: Windows movie file
- ► `.rm`: RealMedia file

Podcasts

Podcasts are a great way to get a hold of your busy audience, in this fast-paced world. Brainshark is a great place to upload, edit, and send audio files to those on-the-go who are unable to watch an actual presentation.

Valid formats include:

▶ `.mp3`: MP3 audio format

Narrated documents

In addition to narrated slideshow presentations, narrated documents allow you to present in a more formal fashion. Given the flexibility to upload Microsoft Word documents and even Excel spreadsheets, you now have a larger range of materials to distribute at your next showcase.

Its valid formats include:

▶ `.ppt`/`.pptx`: Microsoft PowerPoint slideshows

▶ `.doc`/`.docx`: Microsoft Word documents

▶ `.xls`/`.xlsx`: Microsoft Excel spreadsheets

▶ `.odp`: Open Office presentation format

▶ `.odt`: Open Office document format

▶ `.ods`: Open Office spreadsheet format

▶ `.pdf`: Portable document format

▶ `.txt`: Text file

How to do it...

We will now explore how to create our first presentation. The steps are as follows:

1. Go to `http://my.brainshark.com`.

2. Press the **SIGN UP FOR FREE** link in the top-right corner of the screen, going through the registration process and logging in.

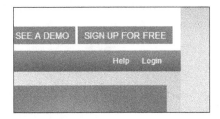

3. Upload your media by pressing the **Upload Content** button. This can be found either on the right-hand side of the screen or the navigation bar.

4. Select your presentation type (that is, PowerPoint, document, video, photo album, or podcast) and press the Upload button.

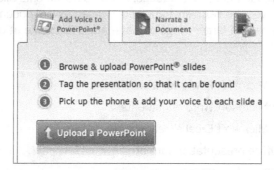

5. Fill out the presentation information while your file is being uploaded. Be sure to change the title to something readable; and ensure that all the relevant fields are filled out. Further details on how to properly categorize or tag your presentations may be found in the *Helping people find your presentations* recipe.

6. Now, we take advantage of Brainshark's unique and powerful audio annotation feature. You can either add audio via a computer microphone or over the phone using the given phone number and presentation code.

How it works...

Brainshark's presentation system allows you to upload and share media online to clients, co-workers, and peers. Its audio annotation system links recorded input from your microphone or phone to sound files that are stored on Brainshark's servers. Then, it is played as the presentation progresses.

There's more...

This section will show a step-by-step process on how to delete and print presentations after creation.

How to delete and print presentations

Note that this process applies to all Brainshark presentations made from this point on.

 Deleted presentations cannot be recovered. Please ensure that you know you wish to delete the presentation before performing the following steps.

1. Press the **My Content** button on the navigation bar.

2. Select the presentation you wish to delete or print.

3. Press the **Edit Presentation** link on the action panel, located on the right-hand side of the screen.

4. Under the left panel, you will find the **Print slides** and **Delete** options.

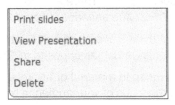

Increasing sales with Brainshark slideshows/documents (Become an expert)

In this recipe, we'll be looking at how to take full advantage of Brainshark's narrated slideshow functionality by following best practices in the presentation design. This will be covered using a list of tips, followed by why these best practices are followed in industry. Lastly, we will look into ways to aesthetically improve existing and future presentations.

How to do it...

The following are best practices that may be used in your own presentations:

1. You should follow Guy Kawasaki's **10/20/30** rule. There shouldn't be more than 10 slides/page, an average presentation should last for roughly 20 minutes, and the font size shouldn't be smaller than 30.

2. If it makes sense, try to customize the layout of your information from the boring, default point form in order to communicate the message in a better way.

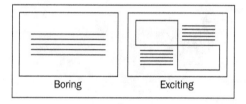

3. Include figures instead of statistics when illustrating data, such as a graph or table.

4. Keep your audience in mind at all times. Do not clutter your presentation with facts that will not interest them.

5. Modify your existing presentations to be Brainshark-friendly, matching slide animations and audio cues properly. There are more tips on how to do this properly in the *Synchronizing slide animations to audio* recipe.

6. When applicable, present the initial sale as a gift rather than a purchase. For instance, "The First Month Is On Us!" as opposed to "Try Us Free For 30 Days".

7. If various slides/pages overlap in material or are related, aim to condense them into one. This will retain the focus of your audience by reducing scope.

8. If your product has already been tested, aim to include social proof (quotes, references, or statistics based on past customers' usage; typically include real names and occupational positions for reinforced integrity) from past customers.

9. Sell benefits to pain points (the pain that your audience is experiencing that your product can help solve), not features. For instance, instead of stating "You can File Your Taxes With Our Software", say "Tired of Filing Your Taxes After an Exhausting Workday? Our Software Does It So You Don't have to!".

10. Where content exclusively describes benefits, include a call-to-action (some button or text meant to prompt a user to click it, leading to a sales conversion) link to purchase on every slide/page.

11. If there are multiple products/plans, make sure to recommend only one to your audience (but have the others available for those who want them).

12. Except for the call-to-action links, aim to minimize website links wherever possible.

13. Whenever possible, try to emphasize how/where the product is made, if it can be used to your advantage. For instance, emphasizing that your manufacturing process is environment-friendly to green customers or that your product was made in Canada for a Canadian audience will aid in sales conversions.

How it works...

This section will show why the steps illustrated in the preceding *How to do it* section are important:

▶ The 10/20/30 rule ensures that you keep the presentation concise and informative, enforcing information constraints. In addition, the 30 font-size rule ensures that all members of your audiences can deal with the visual display of content.

▶ Sometimes, boring and default layouts can be changed to communicate the topic at hand in a better way. For instance, when information is strictly hierarchical, a flowchart might present the content in a better manner.

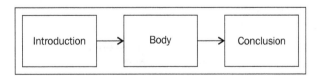

- Statistics are best communicated through visualizations. Figures such as tables and graphs allow audiences to parse information faster and with better comprehension of the issues at hand.

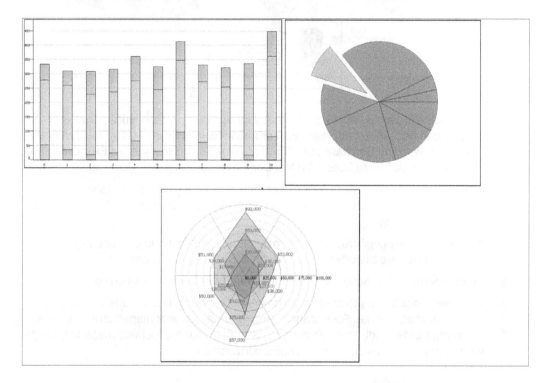

Remember that you should always be selling a product to a particular audience. For instance, if you are selling software to two different audience groups but find that their pain points are different, you should ideally split the presentation into two; one for each group.

- Keep in mind that you will not be presenting personally, so ensure that any audio and visual cues present are properly explained to the audience.

- When presented as a gift, the audience views the initial sale as a window of opportunity instead of a purchase. People are wired to jump at opportunities, leading to impulse purchasing and higher sales.

- There is no need to reiterate information from slide-to-slide. If there is related material across different slides, readers may need to look back at the previous slides to understand the current one.

- Social proof has been proven to be much more effective than self-promotion. Knowing that a user of a similar demographic used the product successfully aids confidence in the buying decision.

- Pain points communicate much easier to buyers than features. Knowing what a product can do is not as powerful as knowing what a product can do to solve their problems.

- By consistently reminding the audience about the call-to-action, you will keep them engaged throughout the sales process. In addition, this ensures that the user does not have to go backwards in the presentation to go through the call-to-action prompt.

- People are often indecisive and do not know what is best for them. By recommending a product to begin with, you eliminate this problem, leading to faster decision-making on impulse and sales.

- Your focus is to sell the product, not distract the audience by directing them away from the presentation. By adding miscellaneous links throughout the presentation, people may leave the slideshow to view them, staying on those sites as a result.

- If people realize that the product aligns with their own personal interests, they will be more willing to support it through a purchase.

There's more...

This section will cover details regarding the basic aesthetic appeal tips:

- Outside images, do not use more than three main colors per presentation.

- Select your animations wisely. Many are tacky and unnecessary.

- Avoid sharp colors.

- Avoid dark backgrounds and distracting objects.

- Ensure that there is sufficient contrast in the text color against the background.

- There shouldn't be more than three font sizes per presentation.

- Any charts, graphs, or tables used must be simple enough for your audience to interpret. On Brainshark, viewers have no one to turn to for their questions in real-time.

- Any call-to-action buttons should aim to have significant contrast and depth differences in comparison to the background for emphasis.

▸ Ensure that you use sans-serif fonts for readability. Examples include Arial, Calibri, Verdana, or Gill Sans MT.

Font to the left is a typical serif font whereas the one to the right is considered sans-serif.

▸ Apply the **6/6** rule. There shouldn't be more than 6 words per point and 6 points per slide.

▸ Avoid using clipart.

Increasing sales with Brainshark podcasts (Become an expert)

Podcasts are now a widely popular way to broadcast information for listeners on-the-go. Given the ability to simply download and listen later, today's society has become adjusted to the convenience that such a medium brings. The following recipe will look into the best practices revolving around podcast design.

An example of a Brainshark podcast

How to do it...

This section will cover best practices alongside podcast recording. The relevant steps are as follows:

1. Ensure that you have a script or outline on-hand during recording.

2. Your audience will want something out of the podcast. Identify what they want and strip off any extraneous details.

3. In addition to step 2, you may find better conversions in reducing the size of your audience and focusing on a niche audience's pain-points.

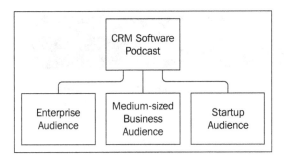

4. If you notice that your audio quality is not up to par, it may be worth identifying the cause, whether it is a noisy recording environment or amateur equipment.

5. Include a downloadable transcript for your audience to ensure that they can trace back to your words in case of audibility issues. We will further discuss how to add attachments in the *Adding attachments* recipe.

6. Podcast recordings should be kept under 15 minutes.

How it works...

This section will show why the steps illustrated in the preceding *How to do it* section are important.

▶ A podcast does not necessarily have to be done in one take. However, having a script or outline in front of you will lower the amount of takes required as it reduces the potential for mistakes. This will allow you to save time in recording and use it towards selling your product instead.

▶ Unlike a slideshow/document, your listeners do not have the option to easily skip irrelevant portions of a podcast. Thus, it is important to align the podcast's message with the needs of your audience.

▶ By splitting up your audience and addressing their individual pain points through different podcasts, you create a more effective message for all of them.

▶ Audio quality is an instant indicator of podcast professionalism. Ensuring that your message is clear removes audibility issues and improves conversions over time.

▶ Unlike a slideshow/document, it is much more difficult for your audience to repeat a section of a podcast to figure out what was said. Having a downloadable transcript ensures that they can look up what was not heard in case a part of the podcast was either inaudible or missed. For more information on how to attach a downloadable transcript, refer to the *Adding attachments* recipe.

▶ The general rule of thumb for podcasts is not to exceed 15 minutes. If you cannot sell your product or portray your message within that span, aim to cut down unnecessary or irrelevant information and try again.

Helping people find your presentation (Should know)

The only thing more important than designing an effective presentation is getting it out there. This recipe looks into the in best practices for search engine optimization and presentation information.

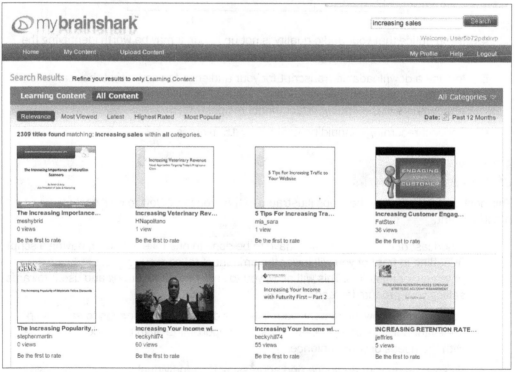

The Brainshark search page

How to do it...

This section will look into how to fill out your presentation information to optimize search rankings:

1. First and foremost, aim to include a title that matches what your audience would use on a search engine. For instance, if you were selling Internet marketing software for small businesses, you could include `Top 10 Ways to Promote Your Product` as the title, as it would be a reasonable search query on search engines such as Google, Yahoo! Search, or Bing. Most importantly, keep this short (at 50 characters or fewer) as Brainshark uses the title in various places for search rank (the rank at which your page shows up on a search engine results page) purposes.

Title:	Top 10 Ways to Promote Your Product

2. Include a brief description (keep this at 100 characters or fewer) of the slideshow. This will show up in search results when keywords that are bound to the slideshow link to the webpage. Try to keep this at a maximum of two sentences.

Description:	How do I promote my product? This presentation helps answer the questions that keep you up at night.

3. Select up to 3 categories that will help represent your presentation. Make sure that they accurately portray your presentation type as incorrect categories can hurt your search ranking if your page is backlinked (when your page is linked from an external source like a blog or magazine website) from a website under different categories.

Categories: Education & Training, Management & Busines

Tag(s):

ⓘ **Select up to 3 Categories**

Current Address:

☐ Arts & Media   ☐ Hobbies & How-To's   ☐ Real
☐ Automotive   ☐ Jobs & Careers   ☐ Sale
☑ Education & Training   ☑ Management & Business Admin   ☐ Scie
☐ Finance & Insurance   ☑ Marketing & Advertising   ☐ Spir
☐ Fun & Entertainment   ☐ News-Politics & History   ☐ Spo
☐ Government & Law   ☐ Non-profit & Charity   ☐ Tech
☐ Health & Medicine   ☐ Personal & Family   ☐ Trav

☑ Enable mobile devices ☐?

Presentation Status:

4. Select tags for your presentation. Note that these will have a negligible effect on search engine results. Tags are primarily for Brainshark's internal search and will help people search for your presentation from within the website. Thus, there are few restrictions around how these should be designed.

How it works...

Search engines such as Google, Yahoo! Search, and Bing deploy spiders, computer programs designed to visit web pages (also known as crawling), and retrieve relevant information for searchers. For instance, a spider may go onto a ski resort website in order to retrieve specific keywords such as the location of the resort, the category of the website (recreation, in this case), and its name. All of this information gets indexed and used to decide the ranking of a search result when a user searches for something on the web. This ranking can be positively affected by relevance between the search terms and the indexed keywords or even negatively affected by irrelevance instead. Thus, it is important to ensure that all tags or categories selected previously relate to the presentation at hand. In addition, long descriptions and titles can lead to more specific search keywords, leading to a lesser search ranking.

There's more...

There's no doubt that, alongside search rankings, a little bit of marketing can go a long way. By adding compelling presentation titles, one is able to improve clickthrough rates and sell the product at a much faster pace. This section will delve into this concept briefly.

Compelling presentation titles

Titles of Brainshark presentations have the strongest effect on search engines and Brainshark's internal search capability. Thus, it is important to master the art of presentation title design in order to increase clickthroughs and sales conversions. To do this, you'll need to find out what keeps your audience awake at night. What are their pain points and what are they most likely to search up on the Internet to solve them?

▸ Survey your existing customers to find out what pain points you help to solve the most with your product.

▸ In "Pain Killer Marketing", the authors *Henry DeVries* and *Chris Stiehl* found that 12 to 15 personal interviews lead to approximately 80 percent of the available pain points for their respective market. More importantly, you should aim to:

  ❑ Meet their expectations by ensuring that the presentation title matches the content presented. Otherwise, you may find people leaving your presentation a lot sooner than expected.

❑ In addition to meeting expectations, ensure that they can get the information they need as succinctly as possible. If your title is "Top 10 Ways To Get More Customers", your audience should be able to immediately jump to the 10 points and begin reading.

❑ Don't forget to include your product and link it to the presentation description. For instance, assuming we used the previous title and your product was able to get more customers, feel free to include a call-to-action for your product.

Designing mobile-friendly presentations (Become an expert)

With the evolution of cellular devices, people are more accessible via their smartphones than ever before. The ability to design mobile-friendly presentations to ensure that your mobile users are not lost is a great way to keep yourself ahead of the competition. This recipe will cover the best practices in mobile presentation design. We note that these tips are geared towards creating presentations for mobile devices, which is distinctively different from the methods explained previously for desktop presentations.

A screenshot of the Brainshark mobile application

Getting ready

To get started with designing mobile-friendly presentations, you'll need to install the Brainshark mobile application in order to allow for self-testing. This may be done using iTunes, if you have an iPhone or related iOS device, or the Google Play Store if you have an Android phone.

Other supported devices that may view presentations via the website include:

▶ BlackBerry

▶ WebOS

▶ Windows Mobile

▶ Android below 4.03

▶ iOS below 4.0

You should test your presentation on both the web browser and the native application to maximize compatibility across platforms.

How to do it...

We now explore the best practices in designing mobile-friendly presentations. The steps are as follows:

1. Note that cell phones can be as little as 1/10th of the size of a desktop monitor. Thus, design your presentations around this to ensure that your font size is large enough to meet the baseline requirements of mobile devices.

2. Mobile presentations are for on-the-go audiences. Thus, ensure that your information is concise, delivering on what is required. There's no sense in expanding beyond what's required, especially if it hurts readability in the process.

3. Try dividing information into more slides rather than placing it all in one.

4. Use graphics wherever possible to communicate your ideas. Text is often too small for many cell phone users to bother reading. People are visual learners and can often recall images better than facts learned through words.

5. Follow the aesthetic tips in the *Increasing sales with Brainshark slideshows/ documents* recipe as readability matters much more when the device size is smaller.

6. Test your presentation with as many mobile devices as possible to ensure maximum sales enablement across platforms. If possible, test with a BlackBerry first, as its keypad interface forces its screen size to be the smallest amongst mobile devices.

How it works...

Here is a quick reference for comparing the Brainshark mobile app with the mobile web browser version to help illustrate their differences:

Feature	Mobile Web Browser Version	Brainshark Mobile App
Animations	√	√
Video	√	√
Presentation Security	√	√
Guestbook Support	v	√
Player Controls (Pause / Fast-forward, etc.)	√	√
Basic Reporting (View Dates, Device Type)	√	
Enhanced Reporting (View Duration, etc.)		√
Table of Contents		√
Downloadable Attachments	√	√
Input to Interactions (Questions, Polls, etc.)		√
Question Branching		√
Question Feedback		√
Multiple Attempts		√
Answer Randomization		√
SCORM/AICC Compliance		√
Rapid Learning Course Support		√
Completion Criteria		√

We note that, although the mobile web browser version of Brainshark has fewer features and is slower on smartphones, it is also available on many more phones. This is because only devices with newer versions of Android and iOS may download and utilize the native Brainshark app. Thus, it is important to minimize the amount of native-only features that your presentation requires to ensure that all viewers can get the best experience.

Synchronizing slide animations to audio (Should know)

Occasionally, slide animations do not perfectly align with the audio recorded. This recipe will briefly look into how to re-sync audio to ensure appropriate performances.

How to do it...

This section will show a step-by-step process on how to sync slide animations with Brainshark:

1. Press the **My Content** button on the navigation bar.

2. Press the **Edit Presentation** link on the action panel, located on the right-hand side.

3. Under **Manage Audio**, select **Record audio**.

4. Select whether or not you'd like to record using microphone or phone.

5. Click on the Record button and then click on the **Next On-click Animation** button to trigger the next animation. The counter underneath the button will indicate the number of animations left in the slide.

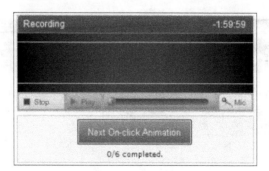

6. Don't forget to add a pause at the end of your audio to ensure a smooth transition into the next slide.

How it works...

Brainshark presentations are designed to play for fixed amounts of time, without user input. As such, it's important to realize that your recorded audio represents the slides' lifetime during the presentation. Ensuring you sync your voice with animations and include pauses will lead to more comprehensible presentations for your audience and better engagement, allowing better sales over time.

There's more...

Sometimes, you may find that a slide does not actually need audio. This may be true in cases where you wish to quickly display a graphic or document that requires no commentary.

Deleting audio from a slide

The following steps will illustrate how to remove audio from your slides:

 Deleted audio cannot be retrieved through Brainshark's support channels or otherwise. Please make sure that you are positive about deleting audio when you follow the given steps.

1. In the left panel, select **Manage slides**.

2. Click on the **Audio** button on the slide that should have its audio deleted.

3. Select **Delete** in the dropdown that pops up.

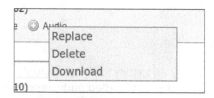

Adding PowerPoint slides (Must know)

Another of Brainshark's strengths comes from its ability to easily integrate existing slides into presentations, leading to faster, automatic conversions. This section will cover how to add additional PowerPoint slides to your presentation.

Getting ready

Adding content slides requires the same type of files as creating your first presentation. Thus, please go to the *Getting Ready* section of the *Creating your first presentation* recipe as a reference for the files required. The following section will cover adding video, documents, and photo slides.

How to do it...

Often, you may want to combine multiple PowerPoint presentations together in an organizational fashion using Brainshark. This section will illustrate the steps to perform this:

1. Hover over the **Add Slides** link in the **What Can I Do Now?** menu and select the **PowerPoint Slide** option.

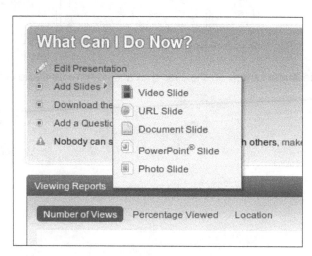

2. Select a file to append to the presentation by clicking on the **Choose File** button.

3. Select between **Append to existing slides** and **Replace existing slides starting at**. The **Append to existing slides** option will place all slides from your uploaded PowerPoint at the end of the presentation. The **Replace the existing slides starting at** choice, however, will require you to select a slide in your Brainshark presentation. This slide and all slides after it will be replaced by the contents of the PowerPoint presentation you choose to upload.

4. Select the **Next** button and the Brainshark conversion process will take place.

5. Once the Brainshark conversion process is complete, it allows you optionally to record audio to go along with the new presentation. Alternatively, you can select the Skip audio generation link at the bottom to move on to the next step.

6. You will be presented with the presentation properties page. Similar to before, you can select **Manage slides** to edit, delete, and add audio to your newly added slides.

How it works...

Note that you are immediately transferred to the presentation slides page. The slide you have added has now been appended to the end of the presentation and you are free to modify it as with a regular slide. Using the arrow buttons to the left, you can re-order the slides to your liking. In order to increase the duration of the slide, add audio that lasts longer than 10 seconds. Once you are done with your changes, press the **Apply** button to change your presentation.

Editing multiple slides

The steps for editing multiple slides are as follows:

1. Under the **Things you can do** menu, select **Manage slides**.

2. You will be brought to a page with all the slides in your presentation. Note that you are given the ability to delete or add audio to each individual slide without leaving the page. This essentially means that you are able to delete or add audio to multiple slides at once. Note, however, that clicking on **Edit** requires you to go to an Edit dialog, reversing your previous changes.

3. Once you have finished deleting or adding audio to your various slides, click on the **Apply** button to apply your changes while staying on the same page. Click on the **Save** button instead to apply your changes and go back to the presentation menu.

Adding URL slides (Become an expert)

One of Brainshark's premiere features is the ability to include Web URL slides for dynamic content. This section will cover how to fully utilize URL slide functionality.

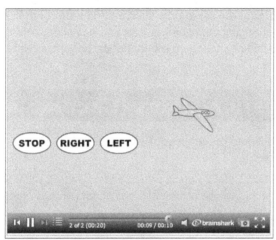

An example of a Shockwave Flash (SWF) URL slide with an airplane animation

How to do it...

The steps to add URL slides are as follows:

1. Hover over the **Add Slides** link in the **What Can I Do Now?** menu and select the **URL Slide** option.

2. Ensure that your website link is working and available to the public. Take the URL of the link and place it in the **Web URL** textbox. Make sure to include the protocol in front of the URL (http://) and assign it a title.

Add URL Slide

To add a web link enter the full URL into the Web URL field below (e.g. enter http://www.domain.com).

Web URL: http://mywebsite.com/pricing.html

Title: Dynamic Pricing Information For Brainshark

---

3. Press the **Save** button.

4. Test your presentation. If you have scrollbar(s) on the webpage and wish to get rid of them, ensure that the dimensions of your webpage are less than or equal to 480 pixels of width and 360 pixels of height.

How it works...

Web URL slides allow you to edit the contents of your presentations on-the-fly by changing your website instead of all your presentations. An example of this is if you have seven presentations all referencing the same pricing information; rather than editing all seven presentations when your pricing changes, you can use web slides and link them to your website. Then, you only need to change the information on your website to update the respective presentations.

Adding question slides (Become an expert)

This recipe will briefly look into the process of adding questions to slides. The following screenshot is an example:

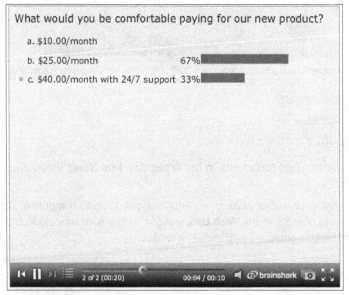

An example of a question slide, with the total audience results to the right side

How to do it...

The steps are as follows:

1. Under the **Things you can do** menu, select **Add a question**.

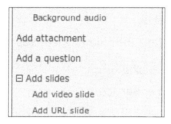

2. Select your question category between either a poll or survey.
3. If your question is a poll, you can select between either multiple choice or true/false questionnaire types.
4. Otherwise, if your question is a survey, select between the following choices:
    -   Multiple choice (choose one only)
    -   Multiple choice (choose one or more)
    -   True/False
    -   Rankings
    -   Ratings
    -   Likert scale

These survey types will be furthered explained in the following *How it works...* section.

How it works...

The variations of polls are fairly self-explanatory. Thus, we will now delve into the various ways to frame a survey.

Survey

Surveys are more complex as they have many more formats to choose from.

-   ▶ Multiple Choice (Choose one only): It is similar to the poll multiple choice format.
-   ▶ Multiple Choice (Choose one or more): It is similar to the previous format but allows for more than one option to be selected. An example for when to use this is when you are asking for a price range on a new product, that is:
    -   "What would you be comfortable paying for our new product?"

        $10.00/month

$25.00/month

$40.00/month with 24/7 support

▸ True/False: It is similar to the poll true/false format.

▸ Rankings: It allows you to order what the customers truly want. An example for when to use this is when you are asking for the ranking of a list of features that your customer wants. That is:

❑ "How would you rank the following features in our product?"

More Affordable Pricing

Friendlier Customer Service

Better Quality

▸ Ratings: It allow your users to rate your options from a scale of 1 to 7 (1 being the highest). This allows you to gauge user interest in various parts of your presentation. That is:

❑ "How would you rate this presentation in the following categories?"

Did the introduction relate well to the presentation?

Did the structure flow well through the presentation?

Was it convincing enough to make you want to purchase our product?

▸ Likert Scale: It is fairly similar to the Ratings format as mentioned previously but is considered the standard for questionnaire type problems. Rather than using a scale of 1 to 7, the Likert Scale uses a predefined scale from 1 (defaults to Strongly Disagree) to 5 (defaults to Strongly Agree). Using the previous example with modified wording:

❑ "How would you rate this presentation in the following categories?"

The introduction related well to the presentation

The structure flowed well through the presentation

The presentation was convincing enough to make me want to purchase the product

There's more...

Question slides may seem only slightly useful at first. You may be wondering how gauging feedback can help you with your products. Additionally, you may be wondering how to properly design a questionnaire. We will explore these topics next.

The importance of customer feedback

By gauging what exactly your customers want, you can improve your product for them and other customers in the industry over time. Customer satisfaction easily converts to revenue retention through loyalty and may even mean additional customer acquisition through referrals. In addition, market trends tend to change without companies noticing it. The simplest way to identify these shifts is to communicate with the customers that experience them. By implementing the changes required, you could be helping out some of your shyer customers as well.

Best practices for questionnaire design

Some of the best practices to follow for questionnaire design are as given:

- Follow the previously mentioned steps to ensure that you are using the correct format across all questions.

- Determine your goal before adding question slides. Then, design your questions and answers as a way to attain the information required to meet your goals.

- Whenever possible, keep your questions and answers as brief as possible. Keep in mind that only a portion of your audience will take the time to read your question slide. Minimize friction.

- Ensure that questions are ordered in a structural manner. Jumping back and forth between topics can be confusing, leading to inaccurate results.

- Test your questionnaire amongst peers to ensure that all questions and answers are clear to the audience.

Adding attachments (Must know)

Often, you may wish to add files to your presentation in order to share content with your audience. Examples of attachments include reports, short audio or video clips, and podcast transcripts. We will cover how to add attachments in this section.

Getting ready

Ensure that your attachment is *NOT* one of the following files:

Restricted file types

- `.com`: COM files; used for issuing commands to the operating system
- `.exe`: Executable files; used prevalently
- `.bat`: DOS batch files; very similar to COM files
- `.vbs`: Visual Basic script
- `.js`: JavaScript

The preceding file types are restricted due to security threats. Also note that the file size of any uploaded attachments must be less than 500 megabytes.

How to do it...

The steps for adding attachments are as follows:

1. Under the **Things you can do** menu within the presentation page, click on the **Add attachment** link.

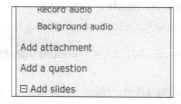

2. Either upload a file from your own computer by pressing the **Choose File** button or provide a Web URL to the file. Then be sure to provide a relevant title to represent the file.

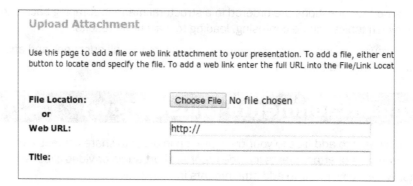

3. Press the **Save** button to include the attachment with your presentation.

How it works...

The preceding steps essentially attach your file to the presentation via the attachment tab. It is essential to allocate a relevant title that is referenced in the presentation so that your viewers can find it easily. There are also various other methods for presenting an attached file, illustrated in the following section.

There's more...

Although the default attachment mode allows your users to download your content without issue, Brainshark has multiple attachment modes to allow different templates for presenting your content. This section will explore these various modes.

Using other attachment modes

The steps for using other attachment modes are as follows:

1. Click on the **Attachments** tab above your presentation preferences.

2. Click on the **Edit** button for the attachment you wish to edit:

3. Select one or more of the following checkboxes to customize when your attachment will be prompted as shown in the following screenshot:

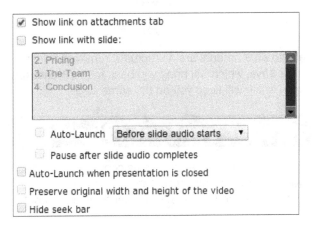

   ❑ **Show link on attachments tab** will display the attachment throughout the presentation for the audience's convenience.

- ❑ **Show link with slide** will only display the attachment on a given slide of your choosing. You can also choose to automatically launch the attachment either before or after the slide's audio is complete. Lastly, you can choose to pause the slide in order to give your audience a chance to download the attachment.

- ❑ **Auto-Launch when presentation is closed** may be an option of interest when you wish to have the users download the attachment immediately after the presentation has concluded. An example of a use case is attaching notes involving your next presentation and launching the download after your current one is done.

Deleting attachments

The steps for deleting attachments are as follows:

1. Click on the **Attachments** tab above your presentation preferences.

2. Click on the **Delete** button for all attachments that you wish to get rid of and confirm with the pop-up dialog that you truly wish to delete the attachment.

3. Note that deleted attachments are not actually removed from the presentation until you press either **Save**, which will bring you back to the **Presentation properties** menu, or **Apply**, which will keep you on the same page.

Embedding your content (Should know)

Brainshark's ability to embed content is as simple as copying a snippet of code to your webpage. Note that you can embed your presentation on multiple pages. This means that you can change the presentation in Brainshark in order to alter the content on all of the said pages.

How to do it...

The following steps will demonstrate how to embed your Brainshark presentation into webpages as a HTML snippet.

To embed your content, go to your presentation properties and click on the **Embed** button next to the **Current Address** textbox.

Note that, there are two options from here. Either select the **Links** tab in order to get a presentation link for sharing purposes or select the **Embed Code** tab to get an HTML snippet for embedding purposes.

Copy-and-paste either the link or the HTML snippet to a webpage. Be sure to test the snippet on multiple browsers and devices so that you are sure that the content is embedded properly. If you find issues during this process, be sure to contact the Brainshark support line to report the bug.

How it works...

Embedding Brainshark content has multiple purposes. For instance, if you use a presentation or document on multiple websites, having the ability to edit the presentation there without having to edit each individual website allows you to streamline changes. In addition, Brainshark's audio annotation system is not something that is easily achieved on a plain website—having the ability to embed the content allows you to fully engage your audience in Brainshark's premiere platform.

There's more...

We will now explore other ways of embedding Brainshark presentations into existing documents or webpages.

QR codes

QR codes (**Quick Response codes**) are used by mobile devices for quick links. By embedding your content using the previous steps, you are using hyperlinks that work better for desktop browsers.

Mobile devices with camera functionality can now take advantage of capturing QR codes that link directly to websites. Each presentation has a unique QR code image that you can save onto printed documents, posters, or even other presentations.

Podcasts

You may also choose to directly link your customers to your podcast. In order to do this, click on the **Podcast** button next to the **Embed** button:

Within this, you will find a link you can embed again in an HTML document or any other document.

E-mailing your content (Become an expert)

In order to keep in touch with your clients, you may be keeping an e-mail list for subscribers that are interested in your product. This section will investigate how to fully utilize your list through Brainshark's e-mailing functionality.

How to do it...

The following steps will demonstrate how to use Brainshark's e-mailing functionality:

1. Under the **Things you can do** menu, click on the **Share** link.

2. Fill in the fields accordingly, separating e-mail addresses with commas. The **Send me a copy** option will send you an e-mail preview of your message and the **Notify me when this is viewed** option will send you an e-mail once your recipients have received the content.

3. Once you are finished filling the fields, click on the **Send** button to issue the e-mail invitations.

How it works...

Note that all e-mails sent out by Brainshark must comply with the CAN-SPAM act. Requirements include:

▸ You cannot send false or materially misleading information through either the body or subject

▸ If you send e-mail without going through Brainshark, you must ensure you include an opt-out or unsubscribe link

By complying with CAN-SPAM, you ensure that you are not blocked by spambots over time and can better cater to the standards that your customers are already accustomed to.

Sharing your content (Become an expert)

In today's data-driven society, leveraging the power of social media can provide instant gains in sales enablement, leading to higher clickthroughs, conversions, and revenue. This section will cover how to share your content with the world.

How to do it...

The following steps will demonstrate how to share your Brainshark presentations on various social media networks including Facebook, Twitter, and LinkedIn:

1. Under the **Things you can do** menu, click on the **Share** link.

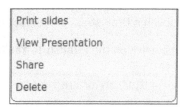

2. Brainshark allows you to share presentations with over a hundred social widgets and networks. Feel free to browse the options by clicking one of the options:

3. Go through the sharing process for the social widget or network you have chosen and confirm that it has been posted. If not, be sure to contact the Brainshark support line to report the bug.

How it works...

Ensure that you are getting an effective return on investment for your content. The social networks for which content typically goes viral are:

- Facebook
- Twitter
- LinkedIn
- YouTube

We will cover publishing to YouTube in the next recipe.

Publishing your content to YouTube (Become an expert)

Since its creation in 2005, YouTube has exploded in growth, now generating billions of views on a daily basis. As a result, it has become one of the world's largest social media sites and a great place to advertise your product and gain users over time. We will explore how to publish your content to YouTube in this section.

How to do it...

We will now investigate how to publish a Brainshark presentation directly to YouTube:

1. On the presentation menu, click on the **Publish To YouTube** link.

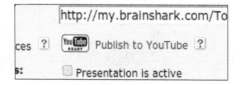

2. Prior to officially publishing your content, take some time to read over YouTube's restrictions and Brainshark's control over your content. This way, you can avoid unnecessary surprises.

3. Grant access to YouTube to allow your video to be uploaded.

4. Once the review process is over, you should find the video uploaded to your YouTube account.

How it works...

Brainshark will go through your YouTube account in order to upload the presentation. By converting each of the slides and audio into video format, it issues a video file that mimics the original. Thus, the video that ends up being uploaded is a separate entity from the Brainshark presentation. This means that changing the presentation means re-uploading it to YouTube.

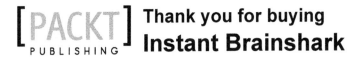

Thank you for buying
Instant Brainshark

About Packt Publishing

Packt, pronounced 'packed', published its first book *"Mastering phpMyAdmin for Effective MySQL Management"* in April 2004 and subsequently continued to specialize in publishing highly focused books on specific technologies and solutions.

Our books and publications share the experiences of your fellow IT professionals in adapting and customizing today's systems, applications, and frameworks. Our solution based books give you the knowledge and power to customize the software and technologies you're using to get the job done. Packt books are more specific and less general than the IT books you have seen in the past. Our unique business model allows us to bring you more focused information, giving you more of what you need to know, and less of what you don't.

Packt is a modern, yet unique publishing company, which focuses on producing quality, cutting-edge books for communities of developers, administrators, and newbies alike. For more information, please visit our website: www.packtpub.com.

Writing for Packt

We welcome all inquiries from people who are interested in authoring. Book proposals should be sent to author@packtpub.com. If your book idea is still at an early stage and you would like to discuss it first before writing a formal book proposal, contact us; one of our commissioning editors will get in touch with you.

We're not just looking for published authors; if you have strong technical skills but no writing experience, our experienced editors can help you develop a writing career, or simply get some additional reward for your expertise.

Building Impressive Presentations with impress.js

ISBN: 978-1-849696-48-7   Paperback: 124 pages

Design stunning presentations with dynamic visuals and 3D transitions that will captivate your colleagues

1. Create presentations inside the infinite canvas of modern web browsers

2. Build presentations that work anywhere, any time, and on any device

3. Build dynamic presentations with rotation, scaling, transforms, and 3D effects

Mastering Prezi for Business Presentations

ISBN: 978-1-849693-02-8   Paperback: 258 pages

Develop JSF web applications with Trinidad and Seam

1. Turns anyone already using Prezi into a master of both design and delivery

2. Illustrated throughout with easy to follow screen shots and some live Prezi examples to view online

3. Written by Russell Anderson-Williams, one of the fourteen experts hand-picked by Prezi

Please check **www.PacktPub.com** for information on our titles

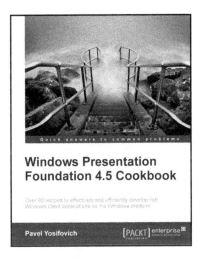

Windows Presentation Foundation 4.5 Cookbook

ISBN: 978-1-849686-22-8   Paperback: 464 pages

Over 60 recipes to effectively and efficiently develop rich Windows client applications on the Windows platform

1. Full of illustrations, diagrams, and tips with clear step-by-step instructions and real world examples

2. Gain a strong foundation of WPF features and patterns

3. Leverage the MVVM pattern to build decoupled, maintainable apps

Instant Prezi for Education How-to

ISBN: 978-1-782163-54-1   Paperback: 60 pages

A fast-paced, practical guide to creating impressive presentations for your students and colleagues

1. Learn something new in an Instant! A short, fast, focused guide delivering immediate results.

2. Learn to create engaging presentations for your students and colleagues.

3. Convert existing PowerPoints into Prezi presentations

4. Create interactive presentations from scratch by adding video, images, and PDFs.

Please check **www.PacktPub.com** for information on our titles